DÉCOLLAGE

First published in 2008 by
Wordsonthestreet
Six San Antonio Park,
Salthill,
Galway, Ireland.
web: www.wordsonthestreet.com
email: publisher@wordsonthestreet.com

British Library Cataloguing in Publication Data:
A catalogue record for this book is available from the British Library.

ISBN 978-0-9552604-6-9

Cover painting: *Gaillimh* © Patricia Burke Brogan
Back cover photograph © Sarah FitzGerald
Cover design: Wordsonthestreet
Layout and typesetting: Wordsonthestreet
Printed and bound in the UK

DÉCOLLAGE

New and Selected Poems

Patricia Burke Brogan

Wordsonthestreet

*To the memory of my parents
Mary and Joseph Phelim Burke*

The author is grateful to the editors of the following where
some of these poems appeared:

Crannóg Literary Magazine
The Salmon Poetry Magazine
West 47 Literary Magazine
Jack Mitchell's Commemorative Magazine
Galway Pirate Women's Magazine
Cork Literary Review
Poetry Ireland Review
Writing in the West (Connacht Tribune)
Cúirt Annual 2006
Salmon Anthology: A Journey in Poetry
The White Page Anthology
Above The Waves' Calligraphy, Salmon Poetry
A Bilingual Anthology of Irish Women Poets, Buenos Aires
I Divas! New Irish Women's Writing Anthology
Women's Work Anthology
The Humours of Galway
Seneca Review, USA
Various Drama Programmes for Eclipsed in the USA and in
Europe
RTE Radio
Galway Bay FM
Poems for Galway Museum

Acknowledgements are due to the following

John O'Donohue, Anne Kennedy, John McGahern, Michael
D. Higgins, T.D., Thomas Kilroy, Gerald Dawe, Carla de
Petris, Mika Funahashi, Sonia Maffina, Gabriella Morisco,
Ginny Garnett, James M. Smith, Caroline FitzGerald, Sarah L.
Roesler, Charlotte Headrick, Eileen Kearney, Karen
Vandevelde, Steve Griffith, Kevin Kerrane, Michael Diskin,
June Favre, Patricia Kennedy, Máire Holmes, John Behan ,
Joan McBreen.

Members of Galway Writers' Workshop.

Members of Writers' Keep.

Galway Education Centre for display of Diptych Collage.

Kenny Bookshops and Art Galleries.

For their advice and support I wish to thank:
My husband, Edward,
and members of my family:
Brendan, Claire, Theresa Ann and Philomena

There is a lovely formation behind the work. It is beautifully honed, but never does an affected pursuit of style defeat the purpose of the poems. The pain is there as evidence of the risk that must be taken in revelation. The eschewing of all evasion requires a price that has to be paid, and we know that a sensitive intelligence, in combining with a released imagination, has made a fine poet.
Michael D. Higgins

you describe the landscape as if your pen were a paintbrush ...
The Plays and Poems of Patricia Burke Brogan
Sonia Maffina,Verona.

Patricia's response to the landscape she inhabits is deeply intuitive. Her aesthetic nerve-ends are out there, feeling, seeing. Her poems are full of visual imagery ... creates through all her senses. She is a consummate artist. Her achievements are multiple. A small woman with a tiny voice, under her skin she is a colossus.
Sheila O' Hagan, Cork Literary Review.

A deep feeling for the spiritual alongside a delight in the sensual world.
Maureen Gallagher

Patricia is an artist to her fingertips.
Caroline Fitzgerald

The pilgrimage that Patricia Burke Brogan brings us on in these vivid poems holds its own ancient healing rhythms. The present is there in all its complexities. The spiritual and the political are side by side.
Rita Ann Higgins

CONTENTS

INTRODUCTION BY KEN BRUEN

'The sun rises, begins to dance
I am netted
in the invisible.'

These lines from Patricia Burke Brogan's *Pascal Night*
hold a particular resonance for me. Patricia is herself, to a
certain extent, netted in the invisible and most certainly in
the un-applauded. Her body of work is quite astonishing,
from her plays to the poems, she is consistently startling,
surprising and above all a true artist. She doesn't look for
the limelight or the glittering prizes, the writing is the
prize.

And what a dazzling gift it is.

Few poets can blend the commonplace with sheer bursts
of pure spirituality and always the language, deceptively
simple and like the best art, has a building effect, grows
on you gradually until you rush back to the pages, see if
what you realize is true, that here is a master-class in
poetry.

She has the sheer majesty of Gerald Manley Hopkins, see
Augusta Gregory, Cygnet on Burnt-out Afternoon and *Celtic
Psaltery.*

And the humility of a Merton, as in *Renewal, The Price* and
Scorched.

Plus she'll break your heart in ways you have forgotten
you could be affected.

The ability to juggle loss and renewal is the hardest feat
of all and she does it profoundly in *Caterina of Siena* and
They Died Young and in the lead poem, *Décollage,* the
searing final lines of that poem

'From that child of Horoshima
I tear off multiple images.
Shadows remain
and I begin again.'

In *Pilgrimage,* the lines it scorches my heart to read

When Brambles' heart stops
I lift his body
and find
his death-sweat
Imprinted
on terracotta tiles.

But this is not a poet who lives in some ivory tower, oblivious to the modern world, the exact opposite, she is all too agonizingly aware of our new prosperous society and never more so than in the shocking *Ladies Day.*
The poem begins with the Galway Races and contains all the brouhaha, excitement and insanity of that event, immerses you totally in the spectacle and then come the lines toward the end.

In Eyre Square at midnight
we wait for an ambulance.
'He'd have murdered me-murdered me gladly.
But I don't want any trouble. I'll be alright to-morrow,'
whispers blonde Magdalene from Birmingham.
Shoeless, she lies face down on the pavement.
Her skull bleeds.

I read her poems, return to her book and I'm given what so few poets ever provide, the mystery of yearning.
And she remains, like most great artists, largely unsung. That is our deepest loss and shame.

Ken Bruen

Galway, September 2008

Paschal Night

In Corcomroe,
a monk cuts into blessed plaster
to reveal this fishing boat,
this fisherman.
Flash of fish scales from his nets
beyond our seeing.

Before dawn
the monk begins
to sculpt limestone harebells
for the altar.
Through this roofless,
doorless abbey,
matins and lauds echo
from ice-scraped grykes
above our hearing.

Bread from cracked fields,
wine from stone pockets.
Invisible credo
on the road to Emmaus.

Beyond a wall of night-cloud
Hale-Bopp drags its sparkling net.
I reach up and search-scrape
into that darkness
to reveal this fire-wound.
millions of years old.

The sun rises, begins to dance.
I am netted
in the invisible.

Pilgrimage

Canvases flat on terracotta tiles,
I scatter torn-up poems
over layers of cloisters, altars
dark doorways of my journey.
Bare feet soaked in blood-colours,
crimsons and magentas,
I walk across this huge collage.

Our dog, Brambles,
stronger
after years of Cardiovet
concealed in butter,
pushes forward
and walks with me.
He barks as I sing
to celebrate his victory
over a greyhound
in Loch an tSáile.

We make paw-prints, footprints.

When Brambles' heart stops,
I lift his body
and find
his death-sweat
imprinted
on terracotta tiles.

Patterns

Rhythm of water
pleats and folds
on river mouth
at Labasheeda.

Pulse of jet-planes
from Moscow, from Boston
shudder above Ardnacrusha.

Rhythm of stone axe
on straight-grained poplar
shaped and carved this canoe
seven hundred years ago.

Heartbeat of a child
swells from a womb-canoe
below Saint's Island.

In Killadysert
the child plays
with mud-patterns
from the estuary.

With a blue crayon
she makes word-patterns,
finds a river poem.

Cygnet on a Burnt-out Afternoon

(June 4, 2004)

Cover me with your wings.
Gather me under your heart-feathers.

Shut out the tumult
of screaming metal birds.
Not our sisters,
not our brothers,
but dark angels spewing terror.

Trapped in this inferno,
we swim underwater
with salmon, mullet and trout
to Augustine's Holy Well.

Marl of mud comforts us
from blasts of flame,
from blasts of blue,
from blasts of dirt-white.
Obscene graffiti
scars flesh of Loch an tSáile
bruises the heart of our dying world.

War-gods, Cromwell, Hitler, Stalin
return to torture carved angels
in the cathedral of St. Nicholas.

Cover me with your wings.
Gather me under your heart-feathers.

They Died Young

I

From Afghanistan to Shannon
war-planes trail white shrouds.
Their undercarriages are filled with body-bags.

Near Labasheeda in County Clare,
Seán 'The Bush' Grady
shapes and varnishes coffins of oak
to cover the aftermath.

Stars and Stripes drape New York
and Washington.
Mourners, hearts darkened by lost loves,
stand to attention for the Last Post.

II

From Gallagh in the west to Dublin's Museum
archaeologists carry aloft one bog-body.
Enemies had twisted willow-rods
around his neck and squeezed until he died.

Near caskets of amber necklaces and gorgets of gold,
his bear-hide shroud trails from umber skin
as he lies, nameless, in a transparent tomb.

In My Next Life

In my next life I'll be a sculptor.
I'll crush cars into cubes,
bash high-rise apartment-blocks
sideways, torch plastic to look
like charred human flesh.

In my next life
I'll assemble a table from recycled news,
display trash in glass dustbins,
collect kitsch from city streets
and make a monument to our dying planet.

Without consent of the powerful,
I'll build bridges,
carve poems
into limestone mountains.

In my next life
I'll polish words in marble and granite
and place them in the open
for everyone to touch.

Décollage

I

From darkness
I drag black refuse bags,
unwind fastenings,
pull out shredded crimsons,
tumble scraps of siennas, burnt umbers
with starched whites and torn ultramarines.

The ghost of Petrushka pirouettes on CD,
criss-crosses, turns head-over-heels,
weaves polytonals for Stravinsky
as I arrange and seal netted colours,
build slabs of ochre,
mix textures coarse and delicate
with ragged memories, forgotten loves.

II

For these anniversaries
I scrape and slice colours,
slit and gouge surfaces,
dig out haunted potato fields
stained by another Holocaust.

From that child of Hiroshima
I tear off multiple images.
Shadows remain
and I begin again.

Caterina of Siena

We walk through a summer
of burnt umbers and ochres,
to find your home.

Here in your father's workshop,
once filled with vats of colour
and dyed fabrics,
we see the metal lantern
you carried to visit lepers,
your scent bottle,
which helped comfort
rotting casualties of plague.

I question Sister Dominic
about your death.
She slices her hand across her neck,
mimes putting her head in a bag.

Your skull lies bandaged
in a golden tabernacle
under these lacquered ceilings,
your body in Rome
near headless sibyls
of the Forum.

Women should keep their heads,
not ask questions.

Lá Fhéile Bríde

I am Brigit,
daughter of Dubthach Saoi
and of bond-woman,
'Little Badger'.

At the feast of Imbolc
Vestal Virgins
crowned with lighted candles
watch over
my Temple of Fire.
Filí and metal-smiths
carry my golden branch
of singing bells

Brideógs and strawboys
drink ale and dance
around my sacred oak.

At the feast of Imbolc
I wrap you in my cloak
of reeds, sunbeams
and snowdrops.
I heal your eyes.
I heal your hearts.

At the feast of Imbolc
I give you my sun-brooch,
woven of the dark
and the light.
I urge you to honour
my earth body, my rivers, wells
and mountains.

I am Brigit
Goddess, Abbess,
Bishop of Cill Dara.

Augusta Gregory

I

Under a rising moon,
spirits from Cregroostha
and Sliabh Echtge
visit your grave,
this limestone writing desk.
Over your carved name
lichens flower with ochre and sienna,
as you listen to Loch an tSáile
croon a requiem for your son
crushed above Tuscan olive groves.

You shall be remembered forever.

II

From Shanwalla to Ballylee
Raftery's blind songs
resound with praise.
You are the copper beech,
the gentian blazing on Flaggy Shore.
You are Coole Lake
filled by underground rivers.
You are the catalpa tree,
the spirit of Kiltartan.

You shall be remembered forever.

*Cregroostha - The original name for Roxborough, birthplace of Lady Augusta
Persse Gregory.
Sliabh Echtge – Slieve Aughty*

Sounds

What words
can tell the pain
in the eyes,
in the face,
in the way
the body moves?
Make new sounds,
sounds never heard
before the first human
stood upright
and all words were pure.
Search for vowels, consonants
to lift and pull
against the force of gravity,
to draw up the skull,
the spinal column,
the long bones.
Find blessed sounds
to banish
that dark shape
waiting
at the foot
of the stairs.

Gaillimh

Bone-dust of Normans
whitens the air.
Bone-dust of armies
darkens the sun.

Bulldozers rape
green flesh of Boherbeg:
Battlefield of
O'Neill and O'Donnell.

Musket-balls fired
from the walls of Forthill
Ricochet along
Bóthar an Iarlaigh.

Birth-cry!

Battle-cry!

Death-cry!

Bastions bared,
dark secrets simmer,
Gaillimh, daughter of Breasail,
drowns in a sea of concrete.

Old battles still rage
through Dúnbun-na-Gaillve,
through this city of soft edges
and mechanical heart.

Lament

A jet-plane embroiders
the sky-tent
over our mirrored city.

****

Rain comes,
pearling concrete edges,
wrapping with gauzes
this wounded landscape.

****

A sun-brooch,
pinned on the shoulder
of the Atlantic
slips
and is lost.

****

All colour gone,
Loch an tSáile is now
a gigantic burial-chamber.
Fossilized beneath
concrete dinosaurs,
our city waits
for future archeologists

Wings

The artist* leans
from flaming windows
of terrorized cities.
He flings white banners
into a bruised sky
and shouts,
'Forgive us for Nagasaki,
Forgive us for Hiroshima,
For Vietnam,
For one billion nuclear deaths.'

His banners become wings
and he flies.

The late John Burke, artist, lived in South Portland, Maine, USA. An exhibition of his peace banners, Shatterer of Worlds, ran at The John and June Allcott Gallery UNC, Chapel Hill September 17 to October 14, 2001 and toured to Amsterdam 2002.

Stop! Stop!

They shout,
'You! Move over there.
No. Over here.'
At seven in the morning
they stamp their feet and shout.

White men in black uniforms
shout at me.
At seven in the morning
they stamp their feet
and shout,
'Move back.
Your passport again.
Stop. Stop!'

White people pass through.
Men and women.
Pale faces look sideways
at me in the airport
of a strange country.
'No room for you.
No room for your unborn child.'

Black men in white uniforms
dig graves for my sisters,
Safiya and Hafsatu.

Who will shout stop
before they stone
Safiya and Hafsatu to death?

Cave

I
My name is Eve.
I lie caged in rock.
Beside me remnants of ochre and fire.
Above me handprints, footprints
of dark ancestors.
I move my left hand,
my left arm.
Pain, searing pain,
screams through me.

II
Deep in the cave
we see her.
On her side,
her flexioned skeleton
protected by stones.
Remnants of ochre and fire around her,
engravings and paintings
by dark ancestors.

We move her carefully,
place her in a glass cage.
Under lights we label her.
'Skeleton of young woman.
Race Protomediterranean.
Lived – 365 B.C. Burial Epipoleolitic.
Cause of Death – Fistulared mastoiditis.
Height one point five three metres.'

III
She hears the throb of music.
Flesh returns to her bones.
Blood dances through her skin.
She hears an avalanche of sounds,
as her eyes open to this cathedral,
this extraordinary cave.

She sees musicians.

A tall man waves a wand
for 'Rite of Spring'.
Flower sounds flow.
Pipes and horns,
threaded rods *zange*
across tendons stretched
on polished shapes.

Their music heals
her pain.

Two pale-skinned dancers
pirouette between stalactites, stalagmites.
One stands on tiptoe,
the other, bird-like, flies.

They do not speak.
They dance.

In the shadows,
beneath the cascade,
other dancers move
in circles along the river
blessing the earth.

IV

She moves her fingers.
She moves her toes.
Her ancestors' paintings
vibrate and dance with her.

She sees him in the orchestra.
She steps out from her cage.

She runs.
She flies.

They do not speak.
They dance.

Miracle

'It'll grow like new potatoes.
You'll have twenty shillings for sweets,'
neighbours' children persuade me.
Under lilies more glorious than Solomon,
a five-year-old believer,
I plant my shining shilling.

'But Jesus was betrayed too!'
Parents comfort
my clay-splattered heart.

'Faith can move mountains.'
I hide my school knitting
in our antique cheese-dish.
'Angel Guardian, please finish
the heel of my sock.'

Eclipsed now by vampire stars,
I dig up my heart-shilling.
Out of that old darkness
I stand at the ocean-edge
and fling-spin my betrayals
across knitted waves-tips
into the miracle of light.

Requiem at Christmas

I sing a requiem for you
at Christmas.
Tinsel and holly pierce my brain.
Not a star
but a twist
of black pain
is pinned
above each shining crib.

As snow, ethereal snow
fades and turns grey,
so your face
loses its light.

You do not say goodbye
at Christmas.
You say,
'Thank you
for keeping watch.'

You die minutes
before I return
to sing for you.
Your eyes are fixed
in surprise
and I know
you can see again.

Heaven

'Draw a picture for me, Daddy!
Swallows home from Africa.
Draw salmon jumping up the river.
Angels and Archangels
Draw Christmas!'

Birds, fish, angels, stars and a frosted donkey
float on coloured space above the stable.

'Draw our old monastery across the road
and don't forget its magic lacy windows!'

He hangs all the magic in a wooden frame
above our bookcase.

******

'Stop those mechanical men. Daddy!
They're taking away our shining road!
Stop those yellow bulldozers!
They're cutting up the monks!
Look, Teeth! Hair! Eyes! Rosary beads!
Hurry, draw the monks. – Draw Heaven!

But --- Where's Heaven now, Daddy?'

Ladies Day

I

'Race Cards, Race Cards, Official Race Cards.'
Three-card-trick men,
live-on-their-wits men.
Race Cards, Race cards, Official Race Cards!'
Tanned ladies clutch tipsy hats
in hope for Press and RTE.

'Jackpot tickets –
Twenty thousand euros guaranteed.'
P. A. crackle, crushed plastic,
reek of horse-dung, armpits, urine, chips and Guinness.

'Giant balloons only one euro.'

'Race Cards, Race Cards, Official Race Cards.'

Swing-boats and chair-o-planes curve
above littered meadows of our Norman castle.

'The moon stood still on Blueberry Hill.
I found my thrill on Blueberry Hill.
On Blueberry Hill, when I found you.'

'The horses are about to leave the parade ring.'
Swinging binoculars and reserved stand labels,
punters, angling at 45 degrees,
rush to the greedy Tote.

'Will the owner of the Rolls Royce
in the enclosure remove it immediately!'

Jockeys in royal blue epaulettes, diamond hoops,
quartered caps, scarlet chevrons and emerald sleeves,
whips and spurs at the ready.

'The white flag is raised! – They're off!'
Under the Corrib Stand, addicted eyes
trained on TV screens, open mouths roaring,
'Come on, Rare Holiday!
Smurfit, can ya not beat O'Reilly!'

Come on, Passer-by. Come on, ya boy ya!'
Neck and neck Kinky Lady and Flashy Buck
take the long bend in the dip.
Sweet-and-Twenty makes a bad mistake.
Come on, Flustered. – A double brandy. Straight!'
Outsider Sagaman wins at twenty-five to one.

In the Champagne Bar bookies celebrate.

Ladies, lips carmined, hair jetted,
high-heeled polyester and viscose
mangle confetti of tote-tickets,
in the penned parade of the fashion mart.
'Passes, please!' Ordinary people turn away
from the Owners and Trainers.

A whip for the champion jockey.

II

Beneath the sapphire waves of Galway Bay
blue sharks swing stealthily, teeth sharpened
for wallets, credit cards, husbands, lovers.

In Eyre Square at midnight
we wait for an ambulance.
'He'd have murdered me – murdered me gladly.
But, I don't want any trouble. I'll be alright to-morrow',
whispers blonde Magdalene from Birmingham.
Shoeless, she lies face down on the pavement.
Her skull bleeds.

'Race Cards, Race Cards, Official Race Cards.'

'I'll be alright to-morrow.'

For a Painter who Died Suddenly

High into the tower he climbed.
He carried Christ on his back.
For that last time he twisted upwards
towards the April night.

When he fell amongst cobalts
and ultramarines,
the Christ-bones offset
on his ivory shroud.

For three days he floated
in his sky-tomb,
as his blood congealed
on stretched boards.

We did not hear the keening of the Magdalenes.
We did not hear the breaking of the bones.
We did not hear the bursting of the heart.
Nor see the lonely flutter of a scarecrow.

They closed him into a pale wooden box
and wedged him under a slabbed hill.

That stony cell in now
his cold cloister.
His painted shrouds
are hanging in the tower.

Tomb

'I've lost him.
I've lost my lover.'
Eyes bruise-burning,
she stares at a blank canvas.

We, her friends, come
to sit on the earth
with her.
We listen to her low keening.

'This will be my last,
my last painting.'
She rocks her body,
digs her fingers into the earth.
'This will be my shroud.'

We offer
chrome yellow,
burnt sienna, vermilion.

'Give me black. Night-black.
Opaque. Without life.
Without light,' she whispers.

'But you taught us
to use a glowing dark.'

We watch.
She takes
a palette knife,
sharp and shining.
She mixes warm umber
with cool ultramarine.

We watch.
She covers
eyes, ears, mouth, nose,
her heart with glimmering dark.
We see her cover the pores of her skin,
as she rolls and curls
and wraps herself
in a luminous tomb.

History

June 1258
In the Banqueting Hall
of the Red Earl
at Dúnbun-na-Gaillve
wine spills
over parchments,
stains battlefields
from Carrickfergus
to Waterford,
from Luichúid
to Furbagh by the sea.

June 1854
The moon
and the Pleiades
pause
as rhythms
of a banjo rise
from crimson petunias
and rusting Crimean cannons
on Eyre Square.

June 1969
From Ballinderry
to Ballymena
viridian hedges
enclose drumming
of railway lines.
Wild roses
entwine
machine-guns
under a lurid sun.

June 1998.
She looks up
at the preserved castle
and says,
'Isn't it strange
how invaders
build walls
like these
to keep the locals out.'

Flint-stone

'I give you the end of a golden string:
Only wind it into a ball, –
It will lead you in at Heaven's gate
Built in Jerusalem's wall.' – Blake

On Sea Lane
I hold a flint-stone in my hand,
chalk crushed under ancient oceans,
stained with crimson of iron.
Bird-shape carved by waves,
ejected as the ice-cap melted,
it resonates with cries
of oyster-catchers and sandpipers
as they skim the tide
and cormorants, wings spread wide,
turning sunwards
to heat their swallowed food.

I place the flint-stone to my ear
and hear Blake's angels sing.
The ghosts of Normans,
who landed on this beach
and built their church of flint-stone,
kneel in prayer.
Canute, attended by his royal court,
returns from shore-line
to join Blake's chorus.
Nelson's warships dip their sails.
Spitfires and Messerschmitts
spiral skywards in salute.

My flint-stone becomes a cello,
a violin, a double bass, a harp
as Parry's opus echoes
and earth revolves on its way to Jerusalem.

Written outside the home in Rustington of Sir Hubert Parry, who composed the music for Blake's Jerusalem. His music reveals to me the layered history of West Sussex.

Luggage

Mary Ann heaves two bags
on to the Galway train.
'Books, books, bagsful of books.
All the time I read. All the time.'

She stares into the murk
of her paper teacup
and opens her heart-book.

'My son, Jason, he's an addict.
He burned his house down,
burned his wife and children too.
He wants me out. Out of my own house.
All night long I read. All night long.'

'Bagsful of books. What kind of books?'
'Mills and Boonses, Mills and Boonses.'

At Tullamore she steps into blackness,
dragging her bagsful of books.
The train pulls away with keening of wheels,
'Mills and Boonses, bagsful of books,
Mills and Boonses all night long.'

Pilgrims

Splodged furze, cadmium and saffron
aflame on viridian thorns, edged with burnt-out-earth,
Spring's guard of honour
for the rushing Galway train.

In Louis Copeland suit, a man,
gold-watched, chunky-ringed hand, mobile to ear,
turns his back on the man with the burnt-out face,
plots his moves in *The Financial Times*.

The man with the burnt-out face,
skeletal torso disguised in washed-out clothes,
takes a vodka bottle paper-wrapped from his back-pack
and with a flaming smile, raises it on high,
offers it.

Thief

(Dedicated to the plagiarists of my stage play Eclipsed.)

Deep in the dark
of her soul-story,
she swims.

His shadow looms.

See him circle,
blind her with camera eyes.

His jaws open.

Listen to her moan-song.

Unable to digest her soul,
he vomits.

But keeps her story.

Triptych

Dawn

Suddenly a river-rock moves,
raises a curved neck,
forms long legs stealthily,
freezes.
The heron stabs the river.

Credo

I hear the tip-tap of crutches
as he moves from darkness
to light candles
under a twisted crucifix.

Teampall Bán

On a full tide
at Dún an Óir,
a baby's skull
floats out
to join the dolphins.

Four Haiku

Cluster bombs crimson
our winged skies over Kabul.
Moycullen heals my bones.

From Valentia's shore
salamander footprints glow.
We step on sea-sand.

Camille Souter paints
herring flames on a white plate.
Picasso eats lobster.

Fly high, my eaglets,
soar away from Sellafield.
Spread Donegal wings.

Spy Wednesday, Paris

There's one star in the sky.

      At the Pompidou Centre
clowns, prostitutes, judges
in Rouault's stained glass colours
hang side by side
with his Homo Homini Lupus.

After two world wars
man is hoist on a gallows,
head sideways,
neck broken, hands open.

Hoards of silver coins
lie dulled by blood
and betrayals.

Above echoing cock-crows
Rouault's Ecce Homo insists,
'They do not know what they do.'

      Man is a wolf to man.

There's one star in the sky.

Maundy Thursday, Paris

*In 1816 the King of England with the Hapsburg Ruler from the Congress of Vienna, wrote to
the Pope asking him to delete the Magnificat from all possible usage, because it spoke the
language of the French Revolution.*

Latecomers, we stand barred
outside the congregation in Notre Dame.
From the vestibule
we peer into stained glass shadows.

With a crash the organ exults from the gallery,
radiance floods the nave.
Vested in white, a multitude of priests
place candles along linen-covered tables
in celebration of Christ's last supper.

The Bishop of Paris begins his homily.

A spirit-woman in long robes
slips through those narrow door-bars.
Alizarin crimsons and ultramarines
glow on her white gown
as she glides past startled ministers
and places a jar of spikenard
low on the marble altar.

The Bishop is silent while the woman chants the Magnificat.

Outside, near the Metro,
a lavender-seller intones the Marseillaise.

Holy Saturday, Paris

In Sainte Chapelle on Ile de la Cité
walls of stained glass off-set royal purples
over sculpted apostles and marble floors.
Lancet windows vault like ballet-dancers,
as stone mullions dissolve in arpeggios of light.

Centuries ago, master glaziers
were dreaming up new colours for this huge reliquary.

Above a crystal tabernacle
blood-stained medallions and fleur-de-lys
glow with his crown of thorns, his splintered cross
carried from Golgotha and Constantinople
to King Louis and Blanche of Castile.

Outside the palace courtyard
gendarmes frisk-search and question all who enter.

Within this luminous tomb,
a trinity of mysteries,
we keep watch for Easter morning.

Cloisters of Alghero

From dark caves above Granada,
where entranced Moors sleep,
Paco Pena calls gipsy voices
to the cloisters of Alghero.

Beneath the Tower of Maddalena
oleanders open crimson ears.
Sand-lilies lift silver trumpets.
In the ancient city of Alghero
bougainvillae stains ochre walls.

Chevrons, circles, embossed triangles,
terracotta calligraphy of strings,
olive, jasmine, lemon elipses,
blood-dried earth of Andalucia
in the cloisters of San Francisco.

Ice and flame, laments and love songs,
dark magic on curving strings,
glow of pink on gold Alhambra
under snows of Sierra Nevada.

Along Via Roma and Via Columbano
from Torre Saint Joan,
above the crickets' soft percussion,
under slanting ilex trees
through the island of Sardegna
flows a red-gold river of flamenco.

They come from that scarred Mountain,
Mountain of Pain. Mountain of Fear.
Ancient people quicken from
shadowed doorways of Nuraghe.

The sleeping youth of Aesculapius wakes
to hear scalloped music.

Phoenicians and Genoese to the Piazza Civica.
Zig-zag Romans on white horses.
After them Catalans and Aragonese.
under the Bell Tower thousands gather,
the Bell Tower of Sancta Maria.

Chevrons, circles, embossed triangles,
terracotta calligraphy of strings,
olive, jasmine, lemon elipses,
blood-dried earth of Andalucia
in the cloisters of Alghero.

The Painting

Velasques de Silva
prepares ochres, burnt umbers, siennas.

He half-closes his eyes.

Brush on canvas,
he places the woman in the foreground
stooped over platters of unleavened bread
and flagons of wine
on her kitchen table.

He curves her shoulders,
slants her body.

She turns her head,
begins to breathe.

Velasques de Silva's heart races.

The woman moves again,
watches through the serving-hatch
as the stranger breaks bread
with men he met on the road.

She murmurs, 'He is risen.'

Velasques de Silva
opens his eyes,
says, 'Deo Gratias.'

Still Life

In bruised shadows
beneath his easel
the cast-offs lie.

Ten days ago,
yellow petticoats uplifted,
they gazed and gazed
and stood on tip-toe
in bare-bosomed ecstasy
with the sun.

One move away on canvas
their earthly lover
shaped them,
stroke by stroke,
in yellow heartbeats.

Neutral limbed and colourless,
dried-up breasts
returning to worm-food,
they'll live in Amsterdam
with next year's sunflowers.

The Price

The woman on canvas
wraps her shawl along Merrion Strand.
Haloed above Dublin Bay,
she chants, 'A penny each the red apples.'

At the auction in the RHA,
De Vere holds up her gilt-framed image.
'I start with two hundred and fifty thousand.
You on the right, Sir,
two hundred and sixty thousand?
Chance of a lifetime this Yeats painting.
Put up your paddles.
Two hundred and seventy thousand
from the gentleman on the stairs?
Going! Going!
Going at two hundred and seventy thousand?
Gone!
Sold at two hundred and seventy thousand.'

Outside on Fitzwilliam Street,
the ghost of Honor Bright
loiters along murky pavements,
earning food for her baby.

Fragments

Ash Wednesday stains my forehead
as I clear dust
from this island etching,
your birthday gift to me.

Under glass,
fragments of earth
float on endless seas,
mirroring your final Easter gift
from that garden of agony.

I light this candle for you.
Its tall flame glows.
Warm wax spills over
into my hands,
fragments of your life.

Renewal

Yellow fillings crumble
reeking of bone-dust,
polyphony of piccolo drills
with hissing of suction,
percussion-drumming, polishing
scraping through tartar,
eyes shut against
that central light,
burning those life-stains,
keeping decay away.

Numbered stones
from ancient arches
on Merchants' Road
 - white painted –
replaced on tarnished buildings.
An orchestra of machines
polishes up history,
keeping death away.

An Teannaloch

A man shuffles into the gallery,
wellingtons squelching on polished floors.
Smell of fish follows him
as he moves among glazed artworks.
He stops and stares
at a painting of Loch Corrib.

He turns to a critic and asks,
'Ar chuala tú riamh an Teannaloch?
I've fished that lake for fifty years.
I've smothered myself in its heart-beat.
I've dived beneath its layered skins
and listened to its soul talk.'
The critic raises an eyebrow
and, glass in hand, walks away.

The painter, in designer-spattered overalls,
stands centre floor.
The man raises his voice,
'Ar chuala tú riamh an Teannnaloch?'
Cameras whirr and flash
as painter and critic pose
for London photographers.

Teannaloch is a local name for ancient Loch Corrib

Scorched

(For Geraldine and Peter)

Geraldine brings me her portrait,
victim of a Christmas house-fire,
'Girl with guitar', oil on board,

My brushstrokes, no longer luminous,
are batiked by brackish smuts,
encrusted with paint-cinders.

Fired aeons ago in earth's cauldron,
pushed up by volcanoes, my chromatic pigments
transformed once again by intensity of heat.

I scrape away scumble on forehead,
on nose, on chin,
uncover highlights on cheekbones.

Through a haze of singed crimsons,
raw siennas, cadmium yellows, ceruleans,
girl and guitar become visible.

Vocal chords and fingers move,
she strums her rock'an'roll rhythms,
we harmonize her song.

Samhain in the Islands

At Ura-bon-e in the East
Mika's mother lights shrine-lanterns
of Mukae-bi fire
to guide her dead ancestors.
She prepares a feast,
toy-horses of aubergine and cucumber,
sings welcome-back songs.

At Samhain in the West,
Oisín and Niamh Cinn Óir
ride across time-oceans
from Tír na nÓg.

Drowned sailors return
from Higan
to celebrate Halloween
with the living.
Past and present merge,
chiaroscuro in charcoal.

When Ura-bon-e has passed,
Mika's mother burns her toy-horses,
lights Okuri-bi fire of farewell.
Niamh Cinn Óir rides eastwards,
Oisín remains with the dead.

According to Mika Funahashi's notes, Higan means Nirvana in Buddhist terminology, but has also a wider meaning, 'the other world 'or 'the place to go'.

Layered Time

At Lynch's Castle,
preserved residence
of Galway's Mayor,*
a family of musicians,
saxophone, trombone,
clarinet and trumpet
play the Beatles', *Yesterday.*

Highlights on brass,
on shoulders, fingers, knees,
rhythm of young bodies,
echo limestone dripstone,
tongue-shaped corvel,
interlaced Runic ornaments.

Under vaulted ceilings,
around that fossiled fireplace,
an orgy of barbequed piglets,
salmon from the Corrib,
barrels of Spanish wine
is indulged by whale-boned ladies
and ermined burghers.

Outside along Shop Street,
tourists from Japan, Estonia, Peru,
the USA, flash digital cameras
on Gothic of invaders.
Puppeteers from Croatia
dramatize legends,
where yesterday it was proclaimed,

'Neither an O nor Mac (or De Burgo)
shall strutte nae strae
thro' the streets of Galway.'

At Lynch's Castle
saxophone, trombone,
clarinet, trumpet
dream in layered time
with ghosts of yesterday.

(Thomas Lynch Fitz-Ambrose was Mayor of Galway, 1654)

Gull

Inspired by Cathal McNaughton's bird photograph, Irish Times October 20, 2004)

Above St. Stephen's Green
a black-headed gull,
wings fanned out,
eyes sharpened,
drops from the June sky,
pins a duckling in its beak
and, red in tooth and claw,
flies away
to a chorus of shrieks
from every feathered throat.

A photograph in *The Irish Times*
shows a black-headed gull,
wings rhythmically spread
against October city's chiaroscuro,
head upright on elegant neck,
reflected in bronze waters,
as it alights in St. Stephen's Green.

A Degas ballet-dancer:
last summer's predator.

Haunted Space

For the premiere of Eclipsed in Punchbag Theatre, Spanish Arch, Galway City on 14th February 1992

By silent music of my blood,
womb-warmth of pressed earth
I know this space.
Haunted by a sense beyond my senses,
I enter this amphora-theatre.
Here on the ocean edge, sky pulses
zig-zag through cerulean openings
to infinity of Cherubim, Seraphim,
as polyphony of doves echoes
along ancient cloisters.

From darkness I call,
'Benedicamus Domino',
to layered generations.
Keening of Magdalenes,
rock 'an' roll of Elvis Presley
counterpoint Poor Clares'
vespers, complin, matins,
as I unwind crimson drapes
from baskets of cremated hearts.

Below De Burgo fireplaces,
Brigit's Holy Well erupts
to resurrect Macha's pagan blessings.
River Corrib applauds Galvia's pregnant chant.
The Atlantic replies, 'Deo Gratias'.

Etched Torso

'To be an artist is to fail, as no other dare fail.' Beckett

In the acid bath
a copper plate
grows dull in turquoise bubbles.
Fumes sway up
from skull thorn-pierced,
shattered shoulder,
torn rib-space.

Acid washed away
in clear water,
she places the etched plate
on a wire-meshed stove.

Gauze-masked, she watches
incense of melting resin rise
above mounds of ink
on double-imaged glass shelves,
orient blue, terracotta,
crimson alizarin,
warm sepia, cerulean.
Incense soars above rows
of glimmering etched plates,
above tins with strange messages,
Laurence of Bleeding Heart Yard,
Charbonnel, Quai Montebello, Paris.
Urbino, Via Sasso, Italia.

Unprotected by opaque bitumen
in the acid bath of resin bubbles,
the etched torso darkens.
Dies.

Grappling with a vision,
she takes a burin and cuts
thin ribbons from tawny metal flesh.

From bundles of soft-textured paper,
Fabriano, Arches, Saunders,
she chooses an ivory sheet.

The printing-press shrieks
as, pushed between heavy cylinder
and bed of the press,
forced between etched lines
and open-bite spaces,
the soft damp paper
takes an inked-up relief.

Disappointed,
she pins the failed image
on a drying line.

Leaving the workshop's
dull glow of copper, neutral of zinc,
she walks out into rain.

A gauzed sky reflects on tarmac.
Between brimming sycamores,
arrows and double lines
tattoo soft skin of earth.

As she walks through water,
through double-imaged clouds,
she finds a Coke tin
distorted by heavy wheels,
a bruised tin man
hangs between earth and sky.

Triangle of Sail

I
Triangle of sail,
white veil of a nun,
tilts and turns
in cloistered waves.
Triangle of sail
glows.
Seaweed scatters,
twists and tangles,
rosary beads abandoned
by a shrouded nun.
Plainchant of ocean,
ellipse of bay,
Black Head bows
to Ballinagall.

II
Triangle of sail.
A silvered fin
tilts to the sun,
glows sapphire and topaz,
when I sing Oratorio
my fins opaline
above the waves' calligraphy.

III
Before I shed
each sequined skin
and slowly
raise my skull
to the sun,
before my lungs
grow to first breath

and I stand upright
on clay and sand.
Before thought,
throat, tongue, lips
form my first word.
Before, eyes open,
I see the moon
through a blizzard of stars
and dawn transfigure
the indigo night.

A silvered fin
from another time,
another life
glows.
A silvered fin,
triangle of sail,
triangle of sail.

Magnificat

The Angelus rings.
I fold my serge habit.
For the last time
I remove the starched half-circle
from my heart.

Not back here again!
No. No. No!
Do I hear the scrape
of scissors cold on my skull,
as that dark-voiced Superior
shears my hair?
Waxed corridors. Silent shapes.
Incense-drenched Magnificat.
Again. Again.

'No vocation, Sister?
You a black novice! No vocation.
You are sure? Sure. Sure.
You mustn't tell. You must wait.
Permission from Rome.
I put you under Obedience.
A Mortal Sin if you tell.'

No Vocation? No Vocation!
Not in here – again!
Must I untie coif and veil,
fold black serge habit,
remove that ring engraved
with Christ Crucified?
Again. Again.

Blessed by the Bishop
in magenta robes?
No. No!
Black robes.

A black dream
Rattle of rosary beads
in a black cloister.
'You mustn't tell.
You must wait!'

The Angelus rings.
I fold my black dream
and leave it
in the convent parlour.

Cell

An ancient door opens.
Stony cloisters.
Dark corridors.
Incense, silence.
A cell with white-washed walls.
Stripped of worldly bronzes,
I put on black habit, white veil.
Soprano-voiced Magnificat
drifts from chapel.
In the refectory
black shapes masticate,
as I read from St. Paul.
'If I have all the eloquence
of men or of angels
and have not Charity,
I am but a booming gong,
a clashing cymbal.'

Under double-lock.
Caged deep
beneath waxed floor-boards,
penitent mothers
in a laundry underworld,
bleach away our sins

Groaning womb-cauldrons
strangle eye-beats, heartbeats.
Huge irons flatten the acid-white sheets
of my Credo
in a black-barred sell.

Letters to Vermeer

I

Galway City,
September 4, 1993

Dearest Jan,
Thank you for writing by return.
Good news at last.
Your Letter-Painting was found in Antwerp.
Yes, that stained glass window
still highlights contours of your lady writer.
Rubies and burgundies glow on your table-cover.
Has the woman, who watches from chiaroscuro,
scrubbed those black and white tiles this morning?
Women don't scrub nowadays, Johannes!

In all your letters you promise to come soon!
You must visit us in this many-textured place.
You must paint our sacred Mullaghmore
before concrete bunkers disguise its magic!
All the blues you love are here, Jan.
Cobalt, indigo, ultramarine, cerulean.
And in April you'll find Gentians!
No, you won't have to grind colours.
Paints come in tubes now.

So please, please come soon.

Love, Patricia

II

Galway City,
September 7, 1993

Dearest Jan,
Please hurry!
This week we dig up skeletons
of outcast laundry women
and sell their graveyards to builder-developers.

Will we steal your painting of our sacred mountain?
In a rush to post,
Love, Patricia.

III

Galway City,
September 12, 1993

Dearest Jan,
Thank you for this drawing of Delft.
I shall treasure it forever.
I'm sorry you were delayed again.
Wish you were here, for to-day
we sail from Rinville to Ballyvaughan.
Turner, your paint-brother, wrapped himself in mast-sheets,
while, storm-battered, he painted sailing ships
in the English Channel.
But do I glimpse your shadow, your stillness, beside
our main sail, as you sketch pucáns and wave-patterns?
No. – I'm only dreaming, Jan!
Beyond Cockle Rock, the sea swells and we move, tiller steady,
towards the Burren, where huge limestone dolphins
reflect in wave-calligraphy.

Every Spring our Burren breaks into flower-miracles
to honour St. Colman, the monks of Corcomroe,
the dead of Poulnabrone and Gleninsheen.
Across the bay the Twelve Pins rise and crumple
as we point first towards Black Head.
Inismeáin to starboard.
Napoleon's Martello Tower and Bell Harbour portside.

Spinnaker folded,
we tack and coast between lurking rocks
through this oyster-packed channel.
A gleoteóg's burgundy sails
blaze under folded limestone.
Alongside Ballyvaughan pier
we put out fenders, fasten ropes,
as Clare music echoes through Aillwee,
where Sidney Nolan paints
to textured rhythms of his ancestors.

I look forward
to the silver light
of your brushstrokes,
to seeing you very, very soon.

Love, Patricia

P.S. Bring sweaters and rain-wear.

Transparent Quickstep

Ghosts are dancing cheek-to-cheek
in Seapoint Ballroom.
Transparent close-knit quick-step waltz
high-lit from a revolving sphere.
Rows of aching bachelors return
to double-doors and stairways.
Rows of girls sparkle
on balconies, at floor-edges.

Dancers without shadows
laugh, sing silently,
while their coffins splinter
in Galway, London, Boston, New York.

Enchanted
we listen as
the Bucharest Philharmonic
tunes strings, percussion and woodwind.

We wait
for Horia Andreescu,
for Hidego Udagawa's violin.

Ghosts and living
silent
as Horia raises his baton.

With Beethoven we mourn Egmont.
Ghosts move to minuet rhythms
as Udakawa celebrates Brahms.
Horia sculpts a lament for Minnehaha,
Dvorak's Largo 'From the New World'.

Horns, bassoons, oboes
from Bucharest, from Tokyo
transcend time-barriers.

Head bowed,
Columbus prays
under these folded hills,
upon these crumpled waters.

Transparent on the balcony,
Peggy, Ambrose and Christopher
watch hearts of the living dance,
hearts of the spirit dance
with the Bucharest Philharmonic
in Seapoint Ballroom.

Make Visible the Tree

This is the Place of Betrayal.

Roll back the stones
behind madonna blue walls.
Make visible the tree.

Above percussion of engines
from gloom of catacombs,
through a glaze of prayer,
scumble of chanting,
make visible the tree,
its branches ragged
with washed-out linens
of a bleached shroud.

In this shattered landscape,
sharpened tongues
of sulphur-yellow bulldozers
slice through wombs
of blood-soaked generations.

This is the place
where Veronica,
forsaken,
stares and stares
at a blank towel.

Four lines from the second stanza are inscribed on a limestone plaque as part of a memorial to The Magdalene Women in Galway City.

Exiles

They remember mountain shapes,
bony masses hulking
from black-umber bogs.
They remember lilac shadows
 moving across bulked rock.

Crushed between skyscrapers,
baked in underground carriages,
deafened in discos,
they remember sky-lakes
rough with tears.
They remember
peppery incense
of saffron furze.

Viridian thorns wrap
granite and limestone,
where haloes wild with colour
dissolve over Maam valley.

Fossiled and transformed
in the ring-round of life,
ancestors' clay
their own clay calls to them.

Slow Time

Floating
northwards
slowly,
crossing the equator,
three hundred
million
years
ago
Galway
swims
in a tropical sea.

The cold comes.
The snow.
Great mountains of ice
move
slowly,
scrape flesh,
fill pockets
with treasures.
Slowly
sinking,
bog-moss enmeshed,
limbs cross-hatched
in a freezing lake.

Northwards
floating,
slowly,
slowly
turning
to
ice.

This Winter

This Winter
we cannot see
the six-twenty train
thread golden beads
through capillaried sycamores,
but we hear its iron pizzicato.
Concrete buildings
new beneath our tricolour
scar the night.
This winter
and all future winters,
unseen from our dinner table,
the six-twenty,
its orange-tipped finger
punctuating the moon,
will stitch
cinnabar of Atlantic
to the fossil-fields of Clare.

Distorted Journey

We cannot swim.
My sisters, my brothers,
we cannot swim in Loch an tSáile.
Cormorants, herons,
we walk on bronze-ruffled ice.
Mirrored in frozen glass,
we move in feathered
choreography
across crystallised space.

Above us
the sun, snow-coifed,
bends to explore
shattered viridian cloisters
on the cold skin
of our sea-lake.

Above you
my sisters, my brothers,
the same sun,
gauzed in orient blue,
is hidden
by metal wings.

We weep for you
our sisters, our brothers
captured in that oil-cage.
We weep
for your burning eyes,
throats scream-swollen,
your charred wings
heavy on an
oil-batiked sea.

We see you move,
amnesiacs, in black ooze.
Smoke fumes,
huge dark anemones
in a bruised sky
distort your journey.

Our sisters, our brothers,
we watch you float
towards the flaming arms
of that oily monster.
Towards that
poison kiss
of man on the
amber lips
of Khafji Sea.

Good Friday, Co. Monaghan 1989

'Where do you come from?'
'Where are you going?'
'Where? Where? Why?'
Soldiers, heavy with guns
circle a checkpoint.

Dry throat silent
Snow-bullets crimsoned,
carmine of rhododendron
stains the green.

Dark voices barter
for a seamless vest
here, where flesh explodes
and that bruised head
looms between the trees.

Snow deepens
its white winding sheet
on Rockcorry, Newbliss
and Annaghmakerrig.

The sun splinters.
Forsaken,
that pierced heart dies.
Day is Night.

Sanctuaries

A June sun offsets
sanctuary-window purples,
saffrons, vermilions
on crypt-grey limestone
in the Cathedral
of Tuaim Dhá Ghualainn.
Dramatic in crimson robes,
the mitred Archbishop
anoints row after row
of young foreheads.
Round scent of oil on skin.
Our shining whiteness
in stony distances.
Kneeling next to me,
Eileen O'Brien picks scarlet varnish
from her fingernails.
In answer to His Grace,
Say the Apostles' Creed, my child!',
she stumbles and forgets
the drilled profession of Faith.
Veils flutter over satin dresses,
while the choir sings,
'Veni, Creator Spiritus.'

But the secretary forgets
to register my name.

Shedding veil and dress
in the afternoon,
from the river bank
I dive into watery greenness.
I swim without fear
through an emerald tunnel.

With pilgrim heron and kingfisher,
with pike and salmon,
I carve watery images.
Miracles of water anoint my body

A strong and perfect Christian,
my fingers break through watercress.
Chant of the river throbs in my ears.
Taste of viridian, incense of
meadowsweet stretching my senses,
I glory in my limbs.
Joy undiminished,
my body is no prison
to contain my spirit.

I swim and swim
with minnows and dearógs,
with brown trout and otters
through cloisters of malachite.
Candelabra of wild iris light the banks.
Water-lilies float with me,
as I salute the clouds.

I write my name in water.

Stone Babies

'Ring a ring o' rosie,
a pocket full o' posy,'
thorn-trees join branches
to shed crimson berries
on a scatter of jagged stones
in this ringfort Killeen.

Do stones keep badgers
from this viridian Limbo?
Do skylarks sing lullabies
for small bones crushed
in unblessed Lisheenduff?
'A-tishoo. A-tishoo. We all fall down!'

No names,
for you are unbaptised,
born out of wedlock,
Will o' the Wisp babies!

Who covers dead babies
with daisy garlands, sings
'Ring a ring o' rosie' with you?
Who decorates small graves with quartz,
with granite fossils, limestone sea-lilies,
with metamorphosed corals?

Outcasts on this river edge,
must you never cross over,
wait in darkness
with strangers?
Will water from Brigit's Holy Well
carry your bone-dust
to Bethlehem?
Or will you, Stone Babies,
sing 'Ring a ring o' rosie' forever?

Three Museum Poems

All framed and exhibited in the New Museum, Galway City with etching 'Gaillimh' 2007

Daughter of Breasail

The woman moves towards the river
to cool her pregnant body.
She steps on limestone
honeycombed by rain.
She lifts her garment
and floats to the Atlantic.
We name her new-born city, Gaillimh.

Explorer

Upon these crumpled waters,
under these folded hills,
his eyes on the stars,
Christopher Columbus prays
for a safe journey
over the edge of the world.

Heads
451 A. D. &1798 A. D.

An alizarin sunset offsets
crimson blood-colours
through museum walls
on this silver casket
cradling skull-bones of St. Ursula
martyred for love of her God.
Mirrored on opposite walls,
the portrait of Wolfe Tone,
who died for love of Ireland.

Fál Dán I

I

Along our garden hedge
a Russian Vine, grape-white, luminous,
echoes ballerina tutus from Moscow, from St. Petersburg.
Berberis, crusted in burgundy frills,
protects nests of blackbirds, goldfinches and robins,
shelters the rosebush - memorial to our dog, Brambles'.
A passionflower raises its crucified heart
above textured rosemary and coriander.
Cobwebs trail magic traps on fennel, mint and sage.

II

Beneath the earth,
a mirror-image hedge,
dark life of meshed roots,
in multi-cultured richnesses,
draws word-colours
from Pushkin, Akhmatova, Amergin, Eibhlín Dubh,
Seamus Dall and Aodhagáin.

Fál - Hedge Dán - Poem

Fál Dán II

I

My blunted shears struggle
to free convolvulus-strangled rosemary,
enmeshed horseradish, spearmint,
oregano, marjoram.
Arum lilies, stamens yellow with pollen,
imprisoned by twisting manacles,
bend their cadenced stems.
Rhythms of fuchsia's blood-clots fall
on ochre clay,
sucked dry by anaemic climbers.

II

My pen squelches on whiteness,
a dissonant baton on minims, crotchets, quavers.
Words tangle and disappear,
rooted in time like the ghosts of swallows.
My song is tuneless,
but I go on scratching,
cutting through to set free
that concerto of light and colour,
that hidden poem.

Diptych in September

In the Burren

Above Castle Gregan's lawn,
within an amphitheatre of folded limestone,
swallows perform their ballet of farewell.
La grace sautée and *pas de deux* fill the air
as a wagtail, in dress-suit,
conducts the orchestra of wind and rain-cloud.

Weather Forecast

Sooty tufts on tree-tops
in Westport woods,
a crows' Press Conference.
Then a myriad of wings swing away
to pattern evening sun and sky
with dark squawks,
but soon return to settle arguments
for one night.

Diptych II

From Alaska by post harebell-seeds
echo aurora borealis, glaciers,
volcanoes, fjords.
I plant them in Galway earth
and close my eyes.

Goldfinches, starving
in the wind from the east,
devour Alaskan seedlings.
I open my eyes to raw umber earth.

Lobelia in November

A single trail of lobelia
from a hanging basket
pushes under the window-sash
to our comfortable kitchen.

One fragile jade stem,
upright against glass,
holds three
pale ultramarine flowers.

Transparent on television
European politicians
discuss
the dispossessed.

The weather forecast
for to-night
is minus three
in Bosnia Herzegovina

Celtic Psaltery

A rare Irish Christian psalter, written on vellum, was uncovered by a bulldozer in a midlands' bog in July 2006. It was described by The National Museum as being between 1000 and 1200 years old and that its survival until now was a miracle.'

From bog dark
a broken prayer
rises.
From tongue of bull-dozer
a calligraphy of psalms
slices through a thousand years.
From candelabra of roots
a blizzard of bog-cotton chants,
Sanctus, Sanctus, Sanctus.
From ooze of fraughans,
from oil of blessed vellum
on treasury of canticles
a luminous voice intones,
Sanctus, Sanctus, Sanctus.
The world stops spinning,
the sun dances
to rhythms of ragged tapestry.

Gospa

(Herzegovina August 2007)

Eyes on summit,
boots against bloodied karst,
stick grappling support,
I scrunch my way
up through pilgrim prayer,
up through war clouds,
up through mountain black,
up through body pain,
up through soul darkness,
up beyond spinning suns,
up beyond world time,
up beyond scientific formulae,
up beyond rational thought.

Rosary rhythms
thousands of thousands
stop.
Throbbing footsteps
thousands of thousands
stop.
Crying babies
stop.
Barking dogs
stop.
Breathing bodies
thousands of thousands
stop,
transfigured
in silence.

Glossary

Aillwee - Aillwee Cave in the Burren, Co. Clare.

Ballinagall - An ancient name for Galway.

Brigit's Holy Well - St. Brigit, Abbess of Kildare and Patroness of Poets, had the gift of healing. Holy Wells were named in her honour.

Imbolc - The Feast of Imbolc was celebrated on 1st February which is also the Feastday of St. Brigit. It was based on the old pastoral lambing and calving season and therefore had powerful fertility associations.

Burren - Karst-like landscape of north Co. Clare.

Corcomroe - Preserved remains of a Cistercian monastery in the Burren.

Dearóg - Small fish.

Galvia - Galvia or Gaillimh, daughter of Breasail, according to tradition was drowned in the River Corrib and Galway City was named after her.

Gentians - Small ultramarine flowers of Alpine origin found in the Burren.

Gleninsheen - Site of a portal tomb in the Burren. A gorget of sheet gold, the Gleninsheen Collar which was found there, is now in the National Museum.

Gleoteóg - A small sailing boat used in Galway Bay.

Killeen - Remains of small cell.

Lisheenduff - Burioal place of unbaptized infants in Co. Galway.

Maam - Valley in Conamara, Co Galway.

Macha - Pagan Goddess.

Tuaim Dhá Ghualainn - The town of Tuam lies in a valley between two shoulder-like hills.

Poulnabrone - Portal Tomb in the Burren.

Will o' the Wisp - A fairy light which dances across Irish bogs at night.

Annaghmakerrig - Residence of the late Tyrone Guthrie, now an artists' retreat.

About the Author

PATRICIA BURKE BROGAN is a painter, poet and playwright. Her etchings have won awards at Barcelona and at Listowel International Biennale 1982. Her collection of poetry, *Above The Waves Calligraphy* and the script of her stage play, *Eclipsed*, were published by Salmon Publishing in 1994. The script of her stage play, *Stained Glass At Samhain*, a companion piece to *Eclipsed*,was published in 2002. *Requiem Of Love, A Monologue for stage* was published by Wordsonthe street in 2006 and launched at the Cúirt International Festival of Literature.

Eclipsed has won many awards including a Fringe First at Edinburgh Theatre Festival 1992 and the USA Moss Hart Award 1994.

To date there have been 70 productions of *Eclipsed* on three continents. *Stained Glass at Samhain* and *Eclipsed* have been translated into Italian. *Eclipsed* has also been translated into French and Dutch.

Clarenda's Mirror, a three-act play, was chosen by the artistic panel of the 4th International Women Playwrights Conference for the Irish Showcase at the Galway Conference in June 1997. A staged rehearsed reading took place in University College Galway.

Her memoir, *Memoir with Grykes and Turloughs*, is a work-in-progress.

Patricia received an Arts Council Bursary in Literature in 1993, a European Script Writers' Fund in 1994, and an Arts Council Bursary in Drama in 2005.

She has won a number of awards for her poetry and her work has been the subject of academic study in a number of universities including *The Power of Visual Elements in Patricia Burke Brogan's Work (University of Delaware, USA)* and *The Plays and Poems of Patricia Burke Brogan (University of Verona, Italy)*

Lines from her poem, *Make Visible the Tree* are inscribed on a limestone memorial to the Magdalenes in Galway City.

Also by Patricia Burke Brogan

Requiem of Love
A monologue for stage
Patricia Burke Brogan
ISBN 978-0-9552604-0-7
56 pp RRP €11.00 pb
Online Price! €9.00

Eclipsed
Patricia Burke Brogan
ISBN 978-0-9552604-4-5
100 pp RRP €11.99 pb
Online Price! €9.99

Log on to our online bookshop to buy this and other titles at
the special online price at:
www.wordsonthestreet.com

Or order from:

Wordsonthestreet
Six San Antonio Park
Salthill
Galway Ireland
Email: publisher@wordsonthestreet.com

Printed in the United Kingdom
by Lightning Source UK Ltd.
133506UK00001B/1-129/P